Bree in the Surf!

By Sally Cowan

T0360231

It was sunny at the beach.

"Put a hat on so you do not get sun burn," said Dad.

Bree put a big hat on her long curls.

"Let's swim!" said Dad.

Bree could see big kids
out in the surf.

That surf looks too big!

"We will not go in
the big surf," said Dad.

Bree was glad.

She did some twists and turns
in the little waves.

A very big wave rolled in
to the beach.

Bree was hurled off her feet!

But then, Bree could feel
Dad grab her.

Bree burst up out of the sea.

Bree got such a fright!

The beach was a blur!

Just then, Bree turned.

Some big surf was rolling in,
with lots of frothy foam on top!

But Bree did not turn
and run to the beach.

She jumped up to get
the wave!

Bree rode the wave!

Her curls flew this way
and that!

But then she got dumped in the surf!

She gulped a lot of froth!

Dad rushed to help Bree.

"That was some big surf!"
he yelled.

Bree lifted her curls back
so she could see.

Then ... she did a big burp!

"I love big surf!"
she said, with a grin.

CHECKING FOR MEANING

1. What happened to Bree when a big wave rolled in to the beach? *(Literal)*

2. Who helped Bree when she got dumped in the surf? *(Literal)*

3. Why do you think Bree loved big surf? *(Inferential)*

EXTENDING VOCABULARY

burst	How is the word *burst* used in the story? What else can burst?
frothy	The foam on top of the sea is described as *frothy*. What is something like if it is frothy? How do you think it feels to touch?
turn	Which words in the text have *turn* as the base? How are the meanings of these words similar to the base? How are they different?

MOVING BEYOND THE TEXT

1. Do you like going to the beach?

2. Would you like to try surfing or body boarding? Why or why not?

3. What do you need to do to stay safe at the beach?

4. Do you think you are like Bree? Why or why not?

SPEED SOUNDS

ar	er	ir	ur	or

PRACTICE WORDS

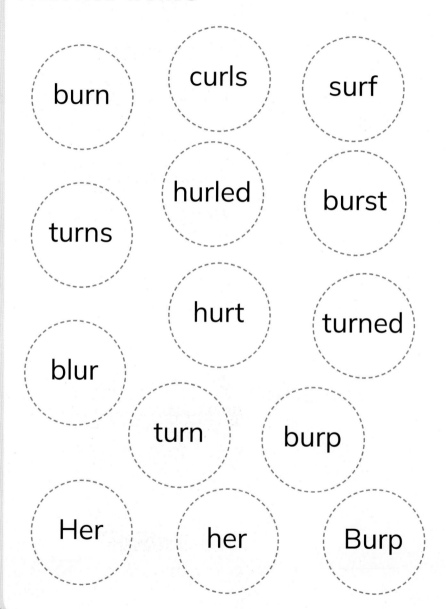

burn

curls

surf

turns

hurled

burst

hurt

turned

blur

turn

burp

Her

her

Burp